(*UN*)LUCKY THIRT33N

Part I

A Collection of Thirteen Short Stories (With Surprise Endings).

Author

Mona Agnihotri

(Alias Monalisa)

Qurate
quratebooks.com

(*UN*)LUCKY THIRT33N: Part I

A Collection of Thirteen Short Stories (With Surprise Endings).

Mona Agnihotri (Alias Monalisa)

Published in 2025

© Published by

qurate
quratebooks.com

Qurate Books Pvt. Ltd.
Goa 403523, India
www.quratebooks.com
Tel: 1800-210-6527, Email: info@quratebooks.com

ISBN: 978-93-58984-57-6

Author's Note

It is said that no one could write shorter short stories than Anton Chekhov, who was one of the greatest 19th century short-story writers from Russia. There is a short story by Chekhov which comprised of *only* four lines, titled - *And She Left…*In this story Chekhov managed beautifully to include all the elements of a short story - the plot, the setting, the characters, the point of view, the conflict, and the resolution.

Chekhov's short stories had surprise endings and thus he is often put on the same pedestal as Guy de Maupassant, H.H. Munro (Saki) and O. Henry who were also world's greatest short-story writers of their times, who wrote short-stories which had surprise endings. Guy de Maupassant was a French short-story writer of 19th century; H.H. Munro (Saki - his penname) was a British writer of 19th century, and O. Henry was an American short-story writer of 19th century. Apart from the commonality in their short stories, and the century that they lived in (19th century), all the four writers had one more commonality - their **short** lives - all of them died before the age of 50, but left an indelible mark in the field of literature and a gaping void to fill.

I was always fascinated by their short stories and so far as I know, I have read them all. This is my tribute to these short-story writers.

The first story in these series - *Who was He!* - is from my late father, who had narrated it to me when he was very ill, and had insisted that I write it for his sake. Hence, this series begins with a **Faith** story.

But before I start these stories, I would like to use a quote – as I always do when I start writing something new! Since most of these stories are God- or Faith-related, I am using a famous quote on God. This one's called – **God's Footprints**. It goes like this (and I am paraphrasing) –

One night a man had a dream – he was walking along the beach with the Lord! Across the sky flashed scenes from his life. In each scene he noticed two sets of footprints in the sand: one belonged to him, and the other to the Lord.

But, he also noticed that during the toughest, lowest and saddest times of his life, the second set of footprints was missing from the sand! This really bothered him, and he questioned the Lord – O, Lord! – he said. - You had said that once I decide to follow you, you will always walk with me. But I have noticed that during the most troubled times of my life, I am walking alone! Your footprints are missing from the sand!

Lord smiled faintly and calmly replied – My son, during your troubled times when you see only one set of footprints, it was then that I was ***carrying*** *you in my arms!*

<u>The Moral</u>: **Never** lose faith and ***Never*** give up hope. God is *always* with you.

Oh, and one more thing, barring the first story, which was my father's creation, as I have mentioned earlier, most of the other stories are true incidences that had happened to me and/or my near and dear ones, including some friends and colleagues. Hope you find your '*faith*' reading these stories.

Dr. Mona Agnihotri

Contents

STORY NO. 1

Who was *He*?

A storm was brewing in the sky. It was a dark and cold night. Suddenly it started raining heavily. A man was staggering to find shelter. The wind was so strong that the man was pushed in the direction the wind wanted him to go. The land upon which he walked was barren, and not a single soul in sight.

The man lifted his head up with great effort to see where he was being taken to by the wind. Far at the horizon he thought he saw a dim light flickering, trying to survive the storm the same way that he was. That dim flickering light gave him tremendous comfort and a feeling of warmth. He wanted to reach where that dim light was flickering as soon as possible. But the wind and the rain were not making it easy. Somehow after what seemed to him like a lifetime, he was able to see the source of that dim flickering light - a hut! He approached the door to the hut and knocked on it.

Inside the hut a family was scared and shivering due to cold and damp weather. The family was poor. There was a mother and her two small children living in that hut. Suddenly there was a knock at the door!

"Mamma," said one of the children, a girl barely eight-years old, *"who could that be?"*

"Don't worry, my child," said the mother, *"God is with us and probably has sent someone to help us!"*

She wrapped herself in a torn blanket and opened the door. A gush of cold and damp wind entered the hut. The mother saw a man standing before her with disheveled hair and beard, and in soaking wet clothes. The man was shivering.

"May I come in, ma'am," he asked politely, and then went on to add – *"I have lost my way in this storm as I am new to this place. Kindly, let me take shelter till the storm is over."*

The man was looking at the mother with such hope and distress in his eyes that she could not say no to him even though she wanted to because she was alone with her two young children.

After a moment of hesitation she said –*"Come in, stranger, but know that my husband will be back anytime."*

The man gave a faint smile, wiped his shoes at the threshold and entered the hut.

Seeing a strange wet man the two children ran behind their mother and started peeking at him.

He looked at the two children and said – *"No need to be scared of me. I am just a passer-by who has lost his way. The moment the storm settles, I will be on my way!"*

"We are very poor, Sir." The mother said, *"hence will not be able to offer you much, but we were just about to have our supper. If you wish, you can join us. You look hungry and tired."*

"Thank you, ma'am," the stranger said, and sat down to eat.

The man looked around the small hut. It had barely a roof on it and the walls looked like they were about to crumble. There was no furniture except for a broken bed with a wobbly leg where the children probably sleep with their mother. There was no sign of a man living with them. The dim flickering light that gave him so much comfort and warmth was actually coming from a lantern which was kept at the center of the hut.

The mother put the food down on the cold floor. It consisted of just dry bread and water.

All of them sat down on the floor. The woman and her children joined their hands and closed their eyes to pray to God and thank Him for the food.

"*Thank you, O Lord, for this food*!" they all said together as the man watched them pray. "*Amen*!"

They opened their eyes. The stranger said to them – "*God will bless you all for offering a person shelter and food when he needed these the most.*"

No one replied to that and they ate their food in silence. Outside the storm was getting worse and making lot of noise as if to compensate their silence. Sound of a nearby river overflowing was also heard. Somewhere the lightning struck and it scared the mother and her children.

It rained and stormed that entire night. The children and the stranger slept but the mother could not sleep as she did not completely trust the stranger. She tried her best to stay awake. The storm was not giving any signs that it would stop soon. The mother muttered – "*O, Lord! Please take care of us! Please, let us be safe. Please, let the storm be over soon*!" She crossed herself and sat quietly for a while.

The mother woke up to the sound of gushing water. She opened her eyes and it was a bright and sunny morning. She suddenly remembered about the stranger and looked that way where he was sleeping, but the stranger was gone! Her children were still sleeping. She started searching for the stranger with her eyes, but there was no sign of him. An uneasy feeling came upon her. She got up suddenly and opened the hut door. She was shocked at what she saw –

The whole land was submerged in water and nothing was floating except for her small hut, which was floating on the water like Noah's Ark!

A sigh escaped her lips – "*O, Lord! Was it **You** with us yesterday night? Was it **You** who saved us!*"

STORY NO. 2

The Calling

Shyamli was not a religious person at all; in fact, one might call her an atheist. She saw so much of ups and downs in her not very long life that she lost all faith in God.

She lost her mother when she was barely seven. Her father never exactly cared for her. She was raised by her maternal grandparents. She grew up thinking that once she grows up she will find her life-partner and they will live happily ever-after. That dream of hers did not last long. Though she did get married, her life-partner turned out to be an abusive drunkard. Hence, here also she did not get the solace that she was searching for her whole life. But a faint hope that someday soon she will become a mother and have a baby of her own to shower all her love upon was still alive inside her heart. Unfortunately, God did not grant her that happiness as well. She waited and waited, until one day she gave up. From that day on she never prayed to God. She stopped visiting temples and celebrating festivals.

The only positive thing she had in her life was her work. Every day in the morning she used to get up with the happy thought that she has her work waiting for her. She had adjusted herself to be a typical middle-class working woman. Weekends were especially hard for her as her drunk, abusive husband used to be at home. She did her household chores with half-heartedness and impatiently waited for the weekend to be over.

A Russian friend of mine once told me that in Russian there is a saying – *'Who is a happy person? – It is the one who every morning looks forward to going to work and every evening looks forward to going back home!'* So, you see, only thing keeping her alive was her work, because for Shyamli the second part of the saying was not true!

It was the month of July and the wedding season was on. Every day some wedding invitation used to come by mail or in person. Shyamli avoided most of them, as she was not very much in favor of marriage. She did not have a very high opinion about marriage. (*Can you blame her!*)

But one day she received a wedding card by post from her hometown Kolkata. She opened it slowly and read the invite – her younger cousin sister, Shubarna, was getting married. Shubarna and she were once very close when Shyamli used to stay with her maternal grandparents. Shubarna's family also stayed in the same house as she was her maternal uncle's daughter. They practically grew up together. They went to school together; shared girly secrets and dreams. This was one wedding invitation that Shyamli could not say 'no' to.

Shyamli called her cousin sister. "*Congrats, Sis. I just got your card.*"

"*You **have** to come, Di*[1]." said Shubarna. "*Get Jiju*[2] *as well.*"

"*Will try. But I will come, definitely.*" Shyamli gave a faint smile. "*Where exactly is your wedding? At dadu's*[3] *place where we grew up?*"

"*No, Di. Dadu's place is in the village; quite inaccessible by road. Baba*[4] *has booked a venue in Kolkata. All the guests who are coming from outside Kolkata will be accommodated at a nearby hotel, including you.*"

---

1. Di – short form of Hindi word – Didi which means elder sister
2. Jiju – short informal form of Hindi word – Jijaji which means sister's husband (brother-in-law)
3. Dadu – Bengali word which means Grandfather
4. Baba – Father in Bengali

Though Shyamli was not very keen to take her husband, she asked for formality's sake.

"My cousin sister is getting married, Shubho. Will you come with me to Kolkata?"

"When?" was all he asked crankily.

"25th July." She replied.

"Nope. Can't come at such short notice. It is already July. You go." He said and walked out of the room.

Shyamli took leave from her work for a few days. She booked an air ticket and was on her way to Kolkata. When she reached Kolkata and was sitting in a taxi going towards the hotel where she was supposed to be staying, she remembered why she loved and missed her hometown so much. The smell of *aloo chop*[5], the abundant sweet shops with *sandesh*[6] displayed proudly at the windows, the sweet *Bangla* language that fell upon her ears whichever place her taxi passed through...

Hotel where she was accommodated was not half as bad. Breakfast was included in the stay; lunch and dinner were at the marriage venue. Shyamli freshened up and went to the venue to meet all the relatives, especially her cousin sister who was getting married.

Shyamli reached a day early for the wedding, and since wedding ceremony was starting from 8 pm the next day, she had the whole morning to herself. She was due to leave the day after the wedding. She decided to spend the morning inside the hotel room. She did not want to go out and see happy cheerful couples with children roaming the streets of Kolkata! She decided to sleep-in late. Shyamli was tired from the journey, so she went to bed early.

She woke up early morning and was shocked to see a black woman in bright red and white *saree*[7] with big red *bindi*[8] on her

---

5. Aloo chop – Potato cutlet in Bengali
6. Sandesh – very popular Bengali sweet
7. Saree – Traditional attire for Indian women
8. Bindi – dot worn by Indian women on the forehead between two brows

forehead and open long black curly hair sitting by her foot on her hotel bed! She smiled at Shyamli and said – *"You come to me, My Child, and I will take away all your pain!"*

Shyamli woke up with a jerk. She was feeling short of breath and was sweating! *'What did just happen?'* she thought to herself. *'Was it a dream?'* Shyamli felt a strange pull as if she is supposed to be some place, but where - that she was unable to explain.

Shyamli got out of the bed, and thought that since she was up she should go to the marriage venue and meet with some other relatives who were coming for the wedding whom she did not meet for what seemed to her like a life-time, including her maternal grandmother – *dida*.

Shyamli's *dida*, a short, thin woman with wrinkles on her face was sitting in a chair at the venue looking at the wedding preparations. The moment Shyamli saw her *dida*, a huge grin came to her face and she went and hugged her *dida* tightly. After some formalities, Shyamli narrated her dream to her *dida*. After listening to the whole story, *dida* said – *"Maa Kali*[9] *called you! You* ***must*** *go to her temple in Dakshineshwar and take her blessings. All your problems will go away!"*

Shyamli realized now that she is supposed to be at Dakshineshwar temple! She immediately booked a taxi. It was already eleven in the morning and the temple remains open only till 1 pm and then reopens at five in the evening, and she also found out that the travel time from Kolkata to Dakshineshwar is around two – two and a half hours in morning-hour traffic. By the time the taxi came, it was almost twelve! Shyamli was ready to move out, so she rushed and sat in the taxi. The driver asked – *"Where to, Didi?"*

"To Dakshineshwar temple!" Shyamli replied not wasting another moment of time as she was already late.

---

9. Maa Kaali – an Indian Goddess who slays demons and protects her worshippers. It is believed about her that her worshippers don't chose her, she chooses her worshippers!

"Not possible, Didi. It is the morning rush-hour. We will have to cross Hawrah Bridge. The temple closes at 1 pm, and it's 12 now! I think you should go in the evening; it opens at 5 pm again." The driver said.

"You just drive; let me do the thinking! I cannot go in the evening; I have a wedding to attend, and tomorrow morning I am flying out. I don't know when I am coming back to Kolkata again." Shyamli said impatiently.

"Didi, I am driving a cab in Kolkata since past 30 years, and have taken people to Dakshineshwar scores of times. One hour to reach there is too short a time. By the time you reach, the temple will be closed!" the taxi driver was adamant.

This angered Shyamli. *"When I am paying the money, and just want you to drive, what is your problem? If the temple is closed, then I will decide what to do next!"*

Taxi driver started the car saying – *"Your wish, Didi. But don't complain if you find the temple closed!"*

That day the entire Hawrah Bridge was empty! The whole way to Dakshineshwar was free of traffic. The road was so dilapidated that the taxi driver looked shocked! The traffic was heavy on the other side of the road. Shyamli not only reached Dakshineshwar temple in 45 minutes, but also was the last person to see Maa Kali's face before the temple shut its doors to visitors for lunch! On the way back, the taxi driver kept looking back at Shyamli with a strange surprise in his eyes, and then he said – *"Didi, I am driving since past 30 years! Never* ***once*** *I found the road to Dakshineshwar empty! Maa actually called you!"*

Shyamli attended her cousin's wedding and went back. Something had changed in her life for the better. Her husband started paying more attention to her. She felt like her life and marriage were getting back on the track. Then she found out that she was pregnant. After nine months of perfect pregnancy she gave birth to a beautiful baby girl. She named her – Kalika! She named her daughter after Goddess Kali.

STORY NO. 3

The Ball of Light

Whosoever said that – **खोजने से तो भगवान भी मिल जातें हैं** – was actually right!

There was an old woman, Sitamma, who was living a lonely life abandoned by everyone. It's not that she didn't have anyone. She did, actually a whole family, but everyone in that family was busy with their own lives, and they all were in a hurry to be somewhere, or be someone, or achieve something! Everyone had forgotten Sitamma. But Sitamma didn't forget anyone, including her dead husband.

Every night she would go to her house's rooftop and sit there in the dark and remember every member of her family one by one. Her son, Dhruv, was far away from her – living in South Africa. He had a wife and two daughters. She remembered him and his family. Her daughter, Dharini, who was married and living in India but in another state. She had a son. Sitamma remembered her. Sitamma also remembered her dead husband and every time she remembered him a faint smile used to appear on her face, but

---

10. खोजने से तो भगवान भी मिल जातें हैं – If you look hard enough, you can even find God! (A Hindi Saying)

soon the smile used to vanish and an expression of sorrow used to take over her face.

Sitamma had a good and happy married life with her husband. She got married when she was barely a teenager and she loved this man - her husband - her whole life. Then one day suddenly he was gone! Cancer took him away from her. Sitamma realized that she had been married to her husband for more than fifty years!

- *Fifty years*! – she sighed. – *It's a lifetime! These days marriages don't even last for fifty days*!

Sitamma started reminiscing - the first time her husband came to see her, the first time she actually saw his face, the love they shared, some fights they had had, and so many memories came flooding back!

Sitamma closed her eyes tightly as if to hold the tears from escaping, but a few managed to fall to the ground near her feet.

- *Why did you leave me alone in this world, my beloved! How will I go on without you*? -

Sitamma sighed heavily, looked towards the sky and started to get up slowly. Suddenly, her eyes fell upon a bright shiny star in the sky. – *That star is unusually bright*! – Sitamma thought to herself, but somehow could not take her eyes off of it.

Soon her stare and admiration for the bright star turned into fear. She could not believe her eyes! The star seemed to be getting bigger and shinier, and she soon realized that it was coming straight towards her with full speed! As the star got closer and brighter it became unbearable to look at it, so Sitamma shut her eyes tightly!

- *"Don't be scared, my dear*! – came a familiar voice – *I am **always** with you!"*

Sitamma was afraid to open her eyes, but the voice sounded so familiar that she couldn't resist. She opened her eyes only to see that her dead husband was floating before her eyes in a ball of light! That scared her so much that she ran downstairs and shut the door to her house. She was panting, and looking up towards the roof.

After a while Sitamma started to relax a bit thinking it was all a dream or maybe, her eyes betrayed her somehow. She wiped her face with her *palloo**[11] and sat down on her sofa. She wondered to herself – *What did I just see? – Is it possible? – Was that my Swami*?*[12]

She looked up again towards the roof. Suddenly, she noticed that the dark staircase started to get lighted-up and the light was getting brighter as if someone or *something* was alighting the stairs! And then she saw the ball of light bumping down the stairs towards her main door. Sitamma started screaming –

- *Go away! Go away! – What* **are** *you*? –

- *Why, I am your husband, Sitey! Don't you recognize my voice*? – came the reply.

Sitamma fainted!

* * *

Sitamma woke up to see that she was lying on the carpet of her drawing room and people are looking at her from outside her window. Some people were shouting, some were crying, and some children were finding it very funny, and so they were giggling.

- *Are you alright, Amma*?*[13] – one of her neighbours asked.

- *What happened*? – Sitamma sat up holding her head.

- *We heard some screams from your house, and came rushing to see you unconscious on the floor*! – replied the neighbor – *Amma, can you open the door? Should we call a doctor*? –

- *Are you hurt, Amma*! – someone else asked

- *Oh, so many questions! – No, I am fine. Just let me get up* –

Sitamma slowly got up. She slowly walked up to the door and opened it. Her neighbours came rushing in. Someone got hold of her, made her sit on her sofa; someone got a glass of water for

---

11. Palloo – a Hindi word for scarf-like loosely-hanging end part of the Indian traditional wear - saree
12. Swami – a word used in India for husband
13. Amma – means – mom; it's an address of respect for elderly women, as well

her. They all looked concerned. Sitamma wasn't used to so much attention, so she said – *I am fine*! – to calm everybody down.

After a while people left.

Sitamma took a deep breath and lay down on her bed. Her head was still aching; she didn't get much of a sleep the previous night. In front of her bed, on the wall was a photo of her dead husband. She kept looking at it and sighed heavily. Then she slept.

When she woke up it was dusk. She slept through the whole day. She was feeling hungry as well. – "*Oh, Lord! Help me.*" Sitamma got up, switched-on the lights because it was getting dark outside. She washed her face and walked towards the kitchen wiping her face with her saree palloo.

- *Sitey*! – came that familiar voice again.

Sitamma turned towards the sofa and she saw the ball of light floating on it. She gasped!

- *Why, Sitey! Yesterday night, on the roof, you were complaining that I left you alone so early! Now that I have come back, you seem to be so afraid of me*! –

This time Sitamma mustered up the courage to reply to the ball of light. She said –

- *You* **do** *know that you are dead*! – she asked in a shaky voice.

- ***Death*** *is a relative concept. The* ***Soul*** *never dies*! – came the reply

- *What do you want....?*" Sitamma asked.

- ***I*** *don't want anything! It's* ***you*** *who is not happy with life. So, here I am.*" - said her dead husband's voice.

- *That means, you are here to stay*? – Sitamma asked with a bit of hesitation.

- *For as long as you want, my Dear.* – replied the voice. – *I realized that I was not fair to you...I left you alone. My whole life you were there with me, for me, but when it was my turn, I left*!

Tears rolled down Sitamma's eyes. She did not know whether she was happy or sad! Then she realized that she was actually selfish for not letting her dead husband's soul rest in peace! This thought made her uneasy. She might have been a lot of things, but she was never selfish; and she wouldn't start being one now.

Sitamma walked back to the sofa and sat down on the carpet beside the ball of light. She looked at it with tears in her eyes, and lifted her fingers to touch it. But her fingers just went through the ball. She looked at it and said with lot of conviction –

- *Swami, I am sorry, I did not let you rest in peace. I am very happy that you came back, believe me, but it is against everything that is right or true. So, I will not hold you back and will always remember you fondly,* ***never*** *complain.* – she took a deep breath and then said – *you can go now, Swami. We had a great life together, and I promise, we will be together again soon.*

The voice was silent for a while, and the ball of light kept flickering. Then as suddenly as it had appeared, it disappeared from in front of Sitamma's eyes.

That night Sitamma dressed herself like a newly-wed woman and went to bed happily. That night after a long time she slept peacefully, as she was at peace with herself, with the world, with her life.

It was morning, the hustle-bustle of life began outside Sitamma's door, but it remained closed. When Sitamma's door did not open till noon, her neighbours started to worry. A few of them knocked on her door, called for her – *Sitamma*! *Sitamma*! – but when they did not get any reply for a long time, the neighbours decided to break her door down.

As they hurriedly entered her bedroom, they saw her lying on her bed dressed in a red *saree*[14] and with a big red *bindi*[15] and vermillion on her forehead! She had a huge smile on her face, and her eyes were closed. She looked peaceful.

A young boy of about twelve went closer to her to wake her up, but as soon as he touched her feet he knew that she was gone!

---

14. Saree - Traditional attire for Indian women
15. Bindi – an adornment worn especially by married women in the middle of their forehead just between their eyebrows.

The young boy started crying and ran back to his mother. People were still standing there wondering what to do when suddenly they saw *two* balls of light appear from nowhere and disappear up into the clear blue autumn sky!

STORY NO. 4

Best Buddies

The war was at its peak. Soldiers were hiding in the trenches, and those that dared to venture out got hit by bullets or were ripped to pieces by an odd bomb falling from the sky! The sound of blazing guns and exploding bombs was unbearable. The soldiers were wet, hungry and exhausted. They wanted nothing more to do with this war that had taken them so far away from their homeland, from their loved ones.

Two corporals named - Pete and Dan were the best of the buddies during such trying times. They managed to keep each-other sane just by being there for each-other. One day suddenly Pete decided to run for it, and he just sprinted out of his trench and ran! He heard his best buddy Dan's voice calling him from behind, horrified - *"**Pete**! Pete, come back! What are you doing?"*

Pete looked back while still running; suddenly he heard a deafening sound right in front of him and the last thing he heard was a loud bang. He lost consciousness the moment he hit the ground.

* * *

Sitting on his wheelchair inside his small apartment and staring at the busy people all day made Pete mad – mad at the war, mad at the people who could walk, but most of all he was mad at himself for losing his leg in the blast. He had simply become a cranky person who had a lot of complaints from life.

Pete was deep in some thought when the doorbell rang. Pete gave out a reluctant chuckle. He dragged his wheelchair towards the main door and asked with reluctance –

- *Who is it? Go away*! –

- *Open the door, Pete*! – came a friendly voice – *I have news for you*!

- *Dan*? – Pete asked.

- *Who else!* – Dan replied.

Pete reluctantly opened the door and turned his back on Dan and said –

- *Why do you* ***keep*** *coming here? Go away! I don't want to hear any more of your stupid plans.*

- *Ok, first of all, my plans are not stupid! Besides, you sit at home all day doing nothing*! – Dan replied.

- *Go away!* – Pete repeated, this time with more conviction.

Dan followed Pete to his bedroom and sat down on his bed. Pete turned towards the bed and saw that Dan was already sitting there. He let out a grunt.

Dan looked excited, and he couldn't hold it in anymore, so the moment Pete turned towards him he blurted out – *We are going for a trip to Himalayas!*

Dan waited for Pete's reaction for a couple of seconds. When there was none, he added –

- *You know,* ***The*** *Himalayas*! –

- *As in…Asia*! – this time Pete replied.

- *A-ha* - Dan nodded with excitement and kept looking at Pete.

Pete stared at Dan for a moment and then replied agitated – *That's the* ***stupidest*** *idea I heard from you so far*!

- *Why*? - Dan looked surprised and hurt.

Pete looked down towards his legs and said - *Duh!* -

Dan got his point, but replied - *Ok, look. We don't have to climb it; just visit.*

- *Nope.* - said Pete and rolled his wheelchair away from Dan.

Dan just kept sitting on the bed feeling a little disheartened. Pete saw this and felt bad. He came back to Dan and said in a soft voice -

- *You know what! Why don't **you** go, and then come back and tell me all about the trip.*

* * *

Dan came back from the trip after two months and was all excited. He couldn't wait to visit his best buddy Pete and tell him all about it. So, one late evening Dan decided to go meet Pete. He rang his apartment doorbell but no one was there. As he waited outside Pete's apartment thinking what to do, an old lady got out of the elevator. As she saw Dan standing in the corridor in front of Pete's apartment, she said politely - *You won't find him this time of the day, son*!

- *Why, ma'am*? - Dan asked her thinking where Pete would go with his one leg.

- *Oh, lately he started visiting this place just round the corner pretty often* - she replied.

Just as Dan was about ask the old lady another question he heard a familiar voice behind him - *Dan*?

Dan turned and saw Pete standing right behind him.

- *Hey, Pete*! - and they hugged.

- *But, wait*! *You are standing*! - exclaimed Dan with joy. - ***How***?

- *Oh, after you left for the trip, I decided to get my life back on track again. I got myself a wooden leg! See!* - and Pete knocked with his fist on his knee area. - *At least I can walk again.*

- *Not bad*! – Dan exclaimed. – *I have some good news too! I met a wonderful girl while I was on this trip!* – Dan looked at Pete for approval.

- *A-ha!* – said Pete and started opening his apartment door. He entered the apartment and switched on the lights. He left the door open for Dan to enter.

- *"A-ha!" that's all you can say about it?* – Dan was hurt.

- *I said – "a-ha" because I met a girl too while you were on your trip*! – said Pete in a matter-of-fact manner.

Dan couldn't believe his ears! – *What!* – he exclaimed. – *That's wonderful! So, when do I get to meet her?*

Soon – said Pete. After a brief pause Pete asked - *And when do I get to meet your girl?*

- *Soon, I guess! Oh, Pete, this girl is amazing! She is smart, pretty and loves adventures! We met during a hike. That's how fate works, I guess. She is from this town only, but I met her in Asia! Imagine, and that too in The Himalayas!* – Dan sounded so excited that Pete did not want to interfere. He kept nodding with a faint smile on his face.

Suddenly Dan exclaimed – *Pete! Why don't we double date? You know, you can bring your girl and I can bring mine! And we meet up someplace. Speaking of places, where* ***are*** *you going these days? Your neighbor said something about some place you go to these days.*

- *That's the place where I met the girl!* – said Pete. – *She is wonderful too, I guess, in her own way.*

- *Ok, then. It's done. We are having a double date!* – Dan exclaimed. – *By the way, what is this place called – you know, where you met your girl?* – asked Dan.

- *The Himalayas*! – exclaimed Pete.

- *What!* – Dan couldn't believe his ears.

- *The Himalayas!* – repeated Pete. - *It's a place not very far from here. It's a wine-n-dine.*

- *Wow! Wine-n-dine by the name of 'The Himalayas'! What are the odds!* – said Dan, - *So you see, Pete, our fates* ***are*** *connected. We are not best buddies for nothing!*

STORY NO. 5

Don’t Judge a Book by its Cover

Robert and Raymond were best friends. They have been best friends since their childhood. Probably, that’s why they have stayed friends because had they met each-other as grown-ups they most definitely would not have liked each-other. That’s because they couldn’t be any more different than two grown-up individuals can be. The *only* thing that was common to both of them was that both their names started with the letter ‘R’.

Robert was outgoing, lively and a happy-go-lucky guy who never took anything seriously in life, and Raymond was a reserved, quiet guy who took *everything* seriously, as if it was a matter of life and death.

Robert had served in the army for a while and was posted to Afghanistan, after which he took retirement from army and settled down in Las Vegas. Raymond by profession was a primary school teacher and was satisfied with his life. He lived in an apartment next door to Robert. They seldom met after Robert came back from the army as their lives were entirely on different paths. Robert enjoyed the night-life, for which Vegas is world famous; Raymond liked to go to bed early, read for a while and then sleep. Another reason was that Robert was an ex-serviceman and had plenty of time on his hands. And since he was single, and not that old, he liked to enjoy his life, mostly at the night clubs of Vegas. Raymond, on the other hand, was a busy school teacher, whose life mostly revolved around his students; but like Robert, he was also still unmarried.

One day a new school teacher joined the school where Raymond was teaching. She was a shy, intelligent woman in her late twenties, who liked to keep to herself. When communicating with other fellow teachers she was extremely polite, but never looked anyone in the eye. She wore these huge glasses with black frame and always dressed in a simple manner; she wore no jewelry. Her name was Sara. Something in her appealed to Raymond so much that he decided to get friendly with her. But this task was not easy, as she was extremely reluctant to let anyone get close to her - physically as well as emotionally. With lot of persuasion, she agreed to have one cup of coffee with Raymond. They met at a nearby coffee shop after school and sat there talking for hours! They clicked instantly, and Raymond realized that this is the woman he would like to marry, for they had many things in common - firstly, they were both school teachers, loved children, and also, by nature, introverts.

Same type of event was unfolding in Robert's life at the same time. The night club Robert liked to visit most had a new dancer. She was vivacious, beautiful and extremely charming. She was always beautifully dressed with lot of jewelry on her. Her smile was more sparkling than her jewelry, though. The night club came alive with her arrival. Her name was Sarah with an 'h'. The first time Robert laid his eyes on her, he was mesmerized. She was such a graceful dancer, and Robert felt that her place was not in this type of a night club. He decided to speak with her personally.

One night after her show was over, Robert sneaked in to her changing room. As she was getting ready to go home, Robert suddenly appeared before her and said:

*- You know, you are the **most** beautiful woman I have ever seen in my life!*

Sarah was startled, but she asked immediately:

- *How many beautiful women have you seen so far!*

Robert was taken aback. He stuttered:

- *No, no....you misunderstood me...*

Sarah started giggling, and said – *Relax! I was just kidding! It's that you used such a* ***cliché****...I just couldn't help! Do you think it's the first time someone has said that to me?*

Robert felt color rising to his cheeks. He was blushing!

- *My, my! Macho military man blushes too!* – Sarah taunted him.

- *How did u know that I am military...?* Robert was confused.

- *Why, the chain around your neck with your tag!"* Sarah chuckled.

Robert was speechless. He just stood there, frozen. Sarah gave a crooked smile, and left.

Robert was feeling horrible. He was so ashamed! Then he was angry at himself. Why was he so nervous? He had dated so many women; what's so special about this one? The whole night Robert tossed and turned in his bed. He couldn't stop thinking about Sarah. Then suddenly he got up and said to himself – ***This*** *is the woman I want to be with!*

Robert decided to speak to her again. But this time he did not enter the night club. He was waiting outside the club for her show to get over. He decided that he would catch her in the alley and pour his heart out to her. As Robert was waiting in the alleyway for Sarah to come out after her show, he saw three shadows in the alleyway. They were whispering about something and were looking excited. They were also waiting for someone, it seemed to Robert. Suddenly, he saw Sarah coming out of the backdoor of the night club. Before Robert could approach her, the three shadow-figures jumped at Sarah and grabbed her tight. One figure closed her mouth with his big hands! Sarah tried to scream for help, but couldn't. As they tried to drag Sarah to their car parked nearby, Robert ran towards them and started kicking them mercilessly. Robert was tall and masculine, and having served in the army gave him additional benefit. Unable to take his blows, the three scrawny figures dropped Sarah and ran away. Sarah was scared to death; she was shaking badly! Robert took her in his arms and put her in his car and started driving.

- *Where to?* – he asked her.

Sarah was too dumbfound! Robert looked her way and realized that she was in a stupor, so this time he shouted her name – ***Sarah!***

That broke her stupor. She looked at Robert and started crying hysterically.

- *Sarah, please calm down! You are safe now. You are with me, Robert. Remember me? The 'macho military man' who blushes*!

Sarah suddenly stopped sobbing, and looked straight at Robert. A smile appeared on her wet face. She leaned towards Robert and kept her head on his shoulder, and after a while, slept off. Robert didn't know what to do! He didn't know where she lived; he couldn't take her back to the night club. So, he drove for a while and then decided to take her home.

Sarah slept like a baby, and when she woke up in a stranger's bed, she became restless. She saw Robert sleeping on a chair beside the bed. She recognized him. For a few moments she was calm, then her eyes fell on the wall clock and she became restless again. She gathered herself and rushed out of his apartment, and collided with Raymond who was coming out of his apartment to go to work. Without looking at him she said – *Sorry!* – and rushed out of the building. Raymond stood there for a while. – *Did she come out of Robert's apartment*? – he wondered. But since Raymond was never late for work, he dismissed his thoughts and went to work.

When Robert woke up, he didn't find Sarah in his apartment. At first he panicked, and then he thought to himself – *She must have gone back to her house.* He decided to go meet her at the night club at night. He was feeling hopeful that after the night's incident Sarah would be more than happy to get out of such a life! He was ready to propose to her.

Meanwhile, Raymond reached school. He was very happy. Sara and he had connected very well, and he decided to propose to her in the evening. He decided that he would invite her over to his apartment for dinner and propose to her. He entered the teachers' room and ran his eyes through the crowd, but couldn't find Sara. – *She must have gone to her class* – he thought, - I will see her at lunch then will invite her for dinner.

After the school was over, he went looking for Sara, but found out that she didn't come to school that day. – Hope, she is fine! – Raymond thought. He went home with a confused expression on his face. When he was opening the door to his apartment, Robert was going out of his. They exchanged – Hellos.

Robert was waiting impatiently for the night; he became so restless that he decided to go for a walk. Robert walked for a long time lost in thoughts. Then suddenly he realized that it was dark. He went home, splashed some water on his face, and rushed to the night club. There he found out that Sarah didn't come to work that night. He was disappointed. As he was entering his apartment, he heard Raymond's voice – *Bobby!*

Robert saw Raymond standing at his apartment door. He said – *Yeah, Ray! What's up?*

- *I need your advice...*said Raymond with some hesitation. Robert stopped opening his apartment door and came towards Raymond.

- *I know that we have not been good friends lately, but...I need your advice...since you are good with women.* This made Robert interested. He said – *You know, today even I need someone to talk to. Let's be friends again; share things and feelings like we used to, what do you say?*

This put Raymond also at ease. – *Yes, lets.*

They both entered Raymond's apartment and sat down face-to-face.

Raymond started first – *There's this girl...uh...woman...a teacher in my school. I think I have fallen for her. Her name is Sara, and she is perfect!*

- *Wow!* – said Robert. – *You having a girl problem! Never expected that!*

After a few second's pause Robert continued – *I also met a girl. Sarah...mine's with an 'h'* - He chuckled. Raymond seemed pleased; they were reconnecting. Robert and Raymond, both blurted out together – *I want to propose to her*.....and then both started laughing!

Then they both sat quietly for a while. Suddenly, Robert blurted out – *What if we* ***both*** *propose to our girls at the same time and same place!*

- *That's a wonderful idea!* – said Raymond. – *But today Sara didn't come to school. I am worried. She is not the type to miss school.*

- *Yeah, my girl didn't come to work today either!* – said Robert.

- *Can we find out where they live?* – asked Raymond.

- *Maybe. I can ask around at the night club, you can ask around at your school. School must keep records of their staff, right?* – asked Robert.

- *Right!* – suddenly Raymond's face lit up with hope. He got up and said to Robert – *I will go to school first thing tomorrow morning and find out!*

- *Okay, then. I will go and find out about mine!* – Robert also got up.

- *Let's get their addresses and meet back here tonight.* – said Raymond excitedly, - *then we can go and meet our girls!*

- *Right-O!* – Robert put his thumb up.

When Robert came back late at night, Raymond was waiting for him at his apartment door.

- *What took you so long?* – Raymond said restlessly.

- *My girl works at a* ***night*** *club, remember? It just opened, and I got her address!* – Robert waved a piece of paper which was in his hands.

I got Sara's address from school, - Raymond waved his piece of paper.

- *Then let's go!* – said Robert. After a moment of hesitation he said, - *Do we go together, or separately?*

- *Where does your girl stay?* – asked Raymond. – *If the addresses are nearby, then we can go together.*

Robert looked at the piece of paper in his hand. Raymond did the same. They both blurted out together - *Henderson*!

- *What did you say?* - Raymond tried to confirm.

- *Henderson,* - said Robert. - *Sarah stays there.*

- *Sara stays there too*! - exclaimed Raymond. - *What a coincidence!*

- *Problem solved! Let's go there together,* - said Robert.

By the time they reached Henderson it was dark. Robert said to Raymond - *Let's go to Sarah's house first…you know she was attacked. Some people tried to kidnap her from outside the night club yesterday. I saved her and brought her to my place as I didn't know where she lived.*

- *Oh,* **that** *was Sarah*! - remembered Raymond. *She bumped into me in the morning. She was leaving in a hurry!*

- *You met her?* - Robert was curious.

- *No. She just bumped into me and said 'sorry' and left! I was going to school, so….*clarified Raymond.

Raymond couldn't even finish his sentence when Robert shouted out - *Here it is! Think this is the house.*

They were standing outside an old apartment building. They were still wondering what to do when someone opened the apartment building door and exited. Before the door closed shut Robert and Raymond entered the building. Sarah's apartment was on the second floor. Robert took a deep breath and rang the doorbell. From inside came hurried footsteps, and Sarah opened the door. Robert and Raymond were both dumbfounded.

Robert said - *Sarah!*

Raymond said - *Sara!*

STORY NO. 6

The Woman in Red

Sonya had a tough childhood. She grew up in a poor family struggling for everything in life, from the basic necessities to important things like education, career. She used to watch people around her neighbourhood celebrate festivals like Holi, Diwali with such grandeur and joy, and thank God for their bounty and good life. She ended up hating people, and more so, *God,* as God did not give her any happiness in life! But she always felt a presence near her, as if someone is guiding her through life, a feeling she could never explain and so, kept to herself. Sometimes, it seemed to her that during nights when her parents were asleep, she used to see a female figure moving around in the house. She used to think that it was her mother, so she used to call out – *Maa*! She used to get the reply – *Shhh...beta*[16]. *Sleep, sleep well.*

She finished her education with great difficulty, but managed to land a good job in a respectable company. Sonya was smart, intelligent and ambitious. She trusted her brain and intellect more than anything. She always said to her friends and acquaintances, and to others who dare ask her – *"Do you believe in God?"* – the

16. Beta – Hindi word used to address a child.

same thing that *maybe* there is God, but *she* doesn't need God anymore. She was confident that she did good for herself and her poor parents so far, and she will do the same for the rest of her life *without* any help from God!

Then came an opportunity of a lifetime. She got a job offer from a very successful company, and she decided to take it. But the glitch was that she stayed in Delhi with her elderly parents, and the job was in Mumbai! She decided that she should not let such an opportunity pass by, so she went to her parent's room to reason with them.

- *Maa, Baba*[17]! – she called out to them.

- *Ha, beta*! – came the reply from inside their bedroom.

- *I need to speak with you both*! – Sonya said entering their room.

Her parents were sitting eagerly on their bed. They understood from the tone of her voice that she was excited about something.

- *What is it, my child*? – asked the mother.

- *I got a good job, but....*, Sonya hesitated.

- *It's ok, beta. Say it*, - said the father.

Sonya blurted out very quickly – *It's in Mumbai. I would like to go*. Then she looked at her parents for their reaction. She was relieved to see that they were not looking very adverse.

Father said very calmly – *It's not our place to stop you. After all, your income is supporting this house. If you feel it's an upgrade, then you have our blessings*. And he looked at the mother for her support. Mother was sitting very quietly. She just nodded, and added – *Go*! *Maa Kaali will be with you*.

A few days later Sonya left for Mumbai. Sonya lived her whole life in Delhi. This was the first time she visited another city, that too the '***city of dreams***' – Mumbai. The moment she set a foot on Mumbai's soil, she knew that her life is about to become wonderful. She started working very hard and put her heart and soul into it. Every month she used to send half of her salary home

---

17. Maa, Baba – a form of addressing one's parents in India.

to parents through money order. She was happy; her parents were fine; could life be any more wonderful!

Then she met Arun. He was smart, handsome and an ace employee of the company where Sonya worked. Every female employee doted over him. But Sonya drew Arun's attention because she always seemed too busy to notice him. One fine day during lunch break Arun came to Sonya's cubicle and said – *Hi, Sonya*!

Sonya looked up and was speechless. She stared at him for a while with blank eyes. Arun felt stupid standing there, so he added – *I am Arun. I am your colleague.*

- *No, no, I* ***know*** *that*! – now Sonya felt kind of stupid. She mustered up the courage and stretched her hand to greet him – *I am Sonya.*

He shook her hand and said – *Yes, I know*! And they both started laughing.

Everyone in that room was staring at them, so Sonya stopped laughing and sat down in her chair. Arun said – *What happened*? – Sonya pointed at others and said almost in a whisper – *They are all looking at us*! –

- *So*? – said Arun carelessly, - *we were just laughing, is that a crime*? – he looked at everybody with anger. People who were looking at them, pretended to go about their own business. He turned back to Sonya and said with a smile – *See, problem solved*!

- *How can you be so bold*? – Sonya asked.

- *How can you be so beautiful*! – he answered her question with a question with a smile on his lips. Sonya started blushing.

There was no stopping them from then onwards. After just a month into their dating Arun proposed to her one day suddenly! They were in a restaurant having dinner and Sonya was supposed to go back to Delhi on a leave to visit her parents. - *What*? – She exclaimed.

- *Will you, Sonya Sarkar, marry me*? – repeated Arun.

She stared at him for a while, and then shouted with excitement – *Yes*! *Of course*!

Arun smiled and took her hands in his and clasped them tightly. Sonya was on cloud nine! Arun took out a diamond ring from his pant pocket and slid it softly onto her ring finger. Sonya was elated! She kept staring at the ring, and tears rolled down her eyes. She couldn't wait to tell her parents about this proposal. The moment she came back to her apartment, she called her parents.

- *Hello*! – came her mother's voice from the other end of the receiver.

- *Maa*! – Sonya exclaimed!

- *Sonya, what happened? You got a promotion or something?* – her mother asked excitedly.

- *Better than that, maa.* – said Sonya. – *Arun proposed to me today, and I said "Yes"!*

Sonya had mentioned Arun to her parents already because she never kept any secrets from them. But the matter would escalate so fast, her parents did not expect that. Her mother gave the phone to her father. _ *Hello, Sonya.* – said the father.

- *Baba*! – said Sonya.

- *Calm down, child. What happened*? – the father asked calmly.

- *Baba! Arun proposed, and I said "Yes"!* – said Sonya elated.

- *Don't you think, all this is going too fast, Sonya?* – asked the father.

Sonya's excitement came down. – *What are you talking about? Arun is a wonderful person. Aren't you people happy for me?* – Sonya felt disappointed.

- *We are your parents. Of course, we are happy for you, but...*- hesitated the father, - *...but...* - Sonya tried to finish her father's sentence - *...you are thinking that you will lose me!"*

- *No, my child. We are your parents, we can never lose you. Even if you are physically away from us, you are always in our hearts...*- the father waited for Sonya to say something, but when she didn't, as she was in tears, he added – *I still think, it's too soon. Please take some time to think about your decision. You barely know this guy*! – the father pleaded.

Sonya kept silent, she was holding on to her phone, and was in tears. Realizing that Sonya is upset, the mother took over the phone – *Sonya,* ***beta****, don't be upset. What your father meant to say was that we have not met Arun yet. So, why don't you ask him to come to Delhi with you to meet us?*

This idea Sonya liked. She was excited again – *Okay, Maa! I will ask him to come with me to Delhi! We will be there in a couple of days! Bye, Maa! Say – good night – to Baba for me.* And she hung up the phone.

It was the month of November, and Delhi weather is very nice this time of the year, not too hot and not too cold. Sonya and Arun entered her parents' house in the evening. Arun was given her father's room, and three of them stayed together in another room for the night.

During dinner Sonya's father was scrutinizing Arun. Sonya's mother cleared her throat and said – *So, Arun beta, tell us about yourself, your family....*she didn't even finish her sentence when Sonya's father blurted out – *Do you drink? Do you smoke?*

Arun was taken aback – *No, Sir!*

Sonya said angrily – *Baba! What are you doing? Stop interrogating him!* She got up from the table, and left. Dinner got over abruptly.

That night was hard on everyone. Sonya kept tossing and turning in her sleep. Her parents were sleeping in the same room.

Arun was not asleep either. In the dark he thought he saw a female figure! She was moving around in the house, and specially hovering around his room. Suddenly, he saw her standing right next to his bed! He switched on the lights, and what he saw made him scream! It was a lady in red *saree*[18] with a big red *bindi*[19] on her forehead. She was black, and had black long curly hair and bloodshot eyes, and she was staring at Arun – *You better keep Sonya happy, or else....!* – was all that she screamed, and then she disappeared!

18. Saree – Traditional attire for Indian women
19. Bindi – a decoration usually round in shape put on by women in India in the middle of their foreheads in between the eyes.

Hearing Arun screaming, Sonya rushed to his room. Her parents followed.

- *What happened, Arun?* - Sonya asked.

- *There was this lady in your house, and she was roaming around, and then she....*- Sonya cut him in the middle of his sentence saying - *Oh, Arun. That was just Maa! When I was living here, I used to see my mother roaming around at night too!*

- *I* **don't** *think it was your mother, Sonya!* - said Arun fearfully.

- *I never roam around in darkness,* ***beta****!* - said Sonya's mother.

- *But when I used to call out to you in the darkness, you used to reply back to me, Maa!* - Sonya was very confident.

- *What did she look like?* - asked the father to Arun.

Arun took a moment to recollect, and then said - *She was in a red saree with a huge red bindi on her forehead, and ...she was black with long black curly hair, and red angry eyes! She warned me...*- Arun was breathless.

Sonya's mother and father gave out a chuckle. Sonya looked at them in surprise. Sonya's mother clarified - *That was* ***not*** *a* ***lady****, per se....That was* ***Maa Kaali***[20]*! She has been looking out for Sonya since she was a child! And hence the warning to you because from now on you will be with Sonya.*

Sonya couldn't believe her ears! She thought that there was no God! And all along Maa Kaali was there with her holding her hand all the way! That day she became a believer!

20. Maa Kaali – an Indian Goddess who slays demons and protects her worshippers. It is believed about her that her worshippers don't chose her, she choses her worshippers!

STORY NO. 7

May I Come?

Lata was pregnant with her first child…

Lata was very attached to her maternal grandfather. Since her father died when she was very young, her mother moved back in with her parents - Lata's grandparents - her *nana* and *nani*[21]. Her *nana* was the father-figure in her life. He was a tall, fair, good-looking middle-aged man who also happened to be the *zamindaar*[22] of their large semi-urban village. He was a popular and just ruler of his village and built many hospitals and schools there among many other things. He was considered as next to God in his village. Lata was mesmerized by his popularity, and his white *dhoti-kurta*[23] which he always wore (well, not the same one; he had many), and his white horse that he always rode, and his British rifle which he received after retiring from the services, and many other things. Her *nana* was the best father-figure she could have asked for!

Lata grew up in his care, did well in her studies, was pampered by her *nani* and mother. She was treated like royalty by all those

21. Nana and nani – maternal grandfather and grandmother, respectively.
22. Zamindaar – in the old feudal system in India, a zamindaar was the land-owner.
23. Dhoti-kurta – traditional Indian dress for most men.

serving her grandfather. All-in-all, Lata had a perfect childhood. Then she graduated from a good college, and started working for which she had to leave her village.

Lata met her would be husband, an army officer, while she was working in town where there was an army cantonment. She had this fascination for uniforms and guns, and fell for her would-be husband very quickly. She saw in him the image of her *nana*. Her would be husband was also tall, well-built and good-looking. He also carried a gun along with his army uniform, and she once saw him riding a white horse in the army barricades where he took her for a visit. That did it for her! And when he proposed to her, she was more than ready to say – *"Yes!"*

Now all she had to do was introduce him to her family which comprised only of her *nana* now. She took a leave from her work and went to her village. Her grandparents lived in a *haveli*[24]. It was huge and white as milk. Lata loved roaming around dancing inside the long corridors of the *haveli* when she was a child. Today she was feeling a bit nervous walking down the corridor to go meet her *nana*. Finally, she reached his chamber and gently knocked on the door.

- *Who is it?* – came a feeble voice from inside the chamber. Lata had forgotten how old her *nana* had become. She entered his room. He was sitting on his rocking chair smoking his *hookah*[25]. He looked so old and wrinkly. Lata almost forgot that it had been twenty years since she left home. Her work did not give her much time for vacations. And after her mother and grandmother died, she stopped visiting her village.

- *Nanu*, - she called out for him.

- *Lata! My dearest one! Come!* – exclaimed her grandfather. He tried to get up from his rocking chair, but collapsed back in. She came rushing towards him, and grabbed hold of him. As he relaxed back into the chair, he said with a toothless smile on his wrinkly face – *Look, how grown up you are, and how beautiful, just like*

---

24. Haveli – a mansion
25. Hookah – Indian equivalent of a smoking pipe.

your mother! – After taking a deep breath he added – *Why have you forgotten your* ***nanu****?*

Lata felt a lump rising in her throat. A tear rolled down her eye. She quickly took control of her emotions, and hugged her grandfather. – *Oh,* ***nanu****! How can I ever forget you! You are the best* ***nanu*** *in the world!*

She lay in his lap for a while, and he stroked her soft and silky hair. - *You know, Lata,* - he said suddenly, - *your mother used to lie down in my lap like this when she was a child. I never thought that I would outlive her!* – he gave out a sad sigh!

- *It's ok,* ***nanu****.* – Lata tried to console him. – *I am here for you. And you know what, I have come to take you with me to town. I have a decent apartment. We can live there together.*

- *It's not my age to move around now. I have some unfinished business here to take care of. Once I am done, I myself will ask for your permission to come live with you.* After a pause, he asked – *I know you have come here for a reason, not just to visit your* ***nanu****!*

Lata got up and looked at her grandfather. – *You know me so well,* ***nanu****!* – she said. – *You are absolutely right!* After a moment's hesitation as if to find the right choice of words, she said – ***Nanu****, you know you have been the most important man in my life,…..*Lata felt a bit shy to continue, so her grandfather did – *But now you have found your own important man! Am I right?* – he gave a toothless smile.

- *Oh,* ***nanu****! You do know me so well!* – Lata blushed. – *You are right. Now I want the two most important men in my life to meet each-other. I know you will love him, he is* ***just*** *like you!*

- *Hmm…we will see about that…,* her grandfather said taunting her. And they both laughed.

Lata's grand wedding took place in her village. Everyone was invited. She looked even more beautiful as a bride, and her groom was so handsome that there were a lot of murmurs in the crowd about him looking just like Lata's grandfather when he was his age. Lata's grandfather was also proud that Lata chose a military man. He liked disciplined people, just like himself.

When it was time to give her away, he took Lata's hand in his and whispered in her ears – *I was proud and honored when I gave your mother, my daughter, away! But today I am even more proud and honored to give you away! May you two have a long, blissful marriage!*

Tears rolled down Lata's eyes, and she was sure that she saw tears in her grandfather's eyes too. She had *never* seen him crying before.

At *bidaai*[26], Lata was feeling very sad. It was normal to feel sad during *bidaai*, but Lata was feeling extra sad to part-away from her grandfather, and she didn't know – why? She felt like she is meeting her grandfather for the last time in her life!

She hugged her grandfather tight and pleaded - ***Nanu**, please come with me!*

Her grandfather said – *Don't worry, my child. When it's time I **will** come and live with you. Now go start a new life!*

It had been three months since her marriage. One night she dreamt of her grandfather. He was standing right in front of her looking the way he used to when she was a child, wearing his white *dhoti-kurta*, with a smile on his face, and he said to her – *Lata! May I come and stay with you now?*

- *Of course, **nanu**! Why are you even asking!* – but as she tried to hug him, he disappeared into thin air!

Lata woke up with a jerk! Something was not right! She woke her husband up, and insisted that he take her to her village. At dawn they reached the village only to see a large crowd gathered at the gates of her *nanu's haveli*. Lata's heart sank. She rushed inside pushing people on the way, and reached her *nanu's* chamber where he used to sit and rock in his chair smoking his *hookah*. She saw her *nanu* wrapped in white cloth lying on the floor! She just stood there in dismay! A servant came to her and whispered in her ears:

- *Baby ji, he died in his sleep at night!*

26. Bidaai – the parting-away ceremony of the bride from her family.

Lata collapsed!

She woke up in a hospital bed. Everything around her was blurry. Her husband was sitting beside her, holding her hand. He had mixed emotions on his face. Lata asked feebly - *What happened? My* ***nanu****?*

- *He has passed away, Dear!* - her husband was silent for a moment. As Lata started crying, he softly added - *But all is not lost, Darling!*

Lata looked at him and said - *What?*

Her husband said - *We are pregnant!*

Yes, Lata was pregnant with her first child, and she was *sure* it was her *nanu* finally coming to stay with her! That's why he appeared in her dream as he was dying, so that his spirit lives on in Lata's child!

STORY NO. 8

The Last Appearance

Dogs are considered to be a man's best friend. Have you ever thought – **why**?

Laika was a beautiful German Shepherd dog. It is said that this breed of dogs is very intelligent and highly loyal. Laika was very young when she was adopted by a couple who didn't have kids. They were married for five years. The couple – Nishant and Neelima treated her like their own daughter. Laika was quickly house trained, and she grew up to be a very gentle, quite, and obedient dog. The couple just adored her. All of their neighbours used to ask them that from where Laika got her house training. Neelima used to very proudly say that it was she who trained her with her love and affection, and by treating her like a daughter, not a dog.

Nishant and Neelima was a working couple. They used to leave early in the morning and come back in the evening. Neelima's office was near their home, so it was she who used to come back by 6 pm. Nishant used to come back late, and he had to travel a lot for work. So, it was mostly Neelima who was with Laika at home.

Laika bonded with her human *'mom'* very strongly and was very protective of her. In the absence of the man of the house, she assumed the role of her protector. She never left her *'mom'* alone, and moved around with her everywhere inside the house. And if by any chance anybody entered the house – be it the plumber, the electrician, or any friend especially a male, Laika used to become extra alert.

With her *'mom'*, Laika was a loving, gentle and caring *'daughter'*. Neelima loved singing, and Laika loved listening to her happy, melodious voice. Neelima loved plants and flowers. They had many potted plants in the balcony of their first floor house. Laika used to sit in that balcony and smell the flowers for hours. The house was not very spacious, and Laika slowly grew up to be a huge dog and so she had to be very careful moving around the house. When her 'mom' left for work, and she was alone in the house, she spent most of her time on the bed because it had her *'mom's'* scent! If she had to go, she relieved herself in the bathroom. She didn't touch or damage anything in the house while the couple was gone. Short of talking, Laika was everything that the couple wanted in a daughter.

One day after coming back from work, Laika came running to her to greet her *'mom'* as she opened the door as usual. This was a routine. But, today Neelima said to Laika in a rather strict tone of voice – ***No**, Laika! **Stay**!*

Laika was unable to understand this behavior of her 'mom'! She just sat and stared at her. Realizing that she had probably been very strict with Laika, Neelima turned back and said to Laika:

- *Laika, I am **soooo** sorry!* – and she hugged her, then continued – *It's just that today mama is **not** feeling very well!*

Laika probably didn't understand the words, but she realized from her *'mom's'* tone that she is not herself today. So she followed Neelima to her bedroom, and waited for her on the bed as Neelima went to take a bath. When Neelima came out of the bathroom, she just lay on the bed lifelessly. Now Laika was worried. Her *'mom'* was her whole world. What happened to her?

Neelima got up late evening. She dragged herself to the kitchen. Laika followed her as usual.

- *Sorry, Laiku! I totally forgot to feed you today evening.* – and she caressed her. But food was not that important to Laika right now; she was keenly observing her 'mom's' face as if to ask her:

- *What's wrong, mommy*?

Neelima noticed this and said – *I am fine, Baby. Just, my stomach is hurting a bit*. But then she held her stomach and ran to the bathroom to vomit. This scared both Neelima and Laika!

When Nishant came home from work, he also got worried looking at Neelima. He took her to a doctor. Laika was impatiently waiting for them to come back home. The moment she heard the sound of key turning in the door, she ran towards it. What she saw in their faces confused her more. Nishant helped Neelima sit on the bed, then patted Laika and said – *You know, your '**mommy**' is going to be an actual '**mommy**' soon!*

Mehak was born nine months later. When Neelima went for delivery, Laika was confused. But she waited for her 'mom' to return soon. Nishant's positive behavior put her at ease that all is well. Neelima's mom had come to stay with them during this time, but Laika did *not* like her at all.

After three days, Neelima came back home. Laika ran towards her to show how much she was missing her '*mom*', but she was stopped by Nishant – ***No**, Laika! **Wait**!*

Laika saw a strange bundle in her '*mom's*' hands, and it was moving and strange cries were coming out of it. She tilted her head sideways like many dogs do, as if to understand the situation better. As they entered the bedroom, Laika tried to enter too, but she was stopped at the threshold of the bedroom by Nishant. He said to Laika – From now on Laika will sleep in the other bedroom with '*papa*'.

And so Laika started getting more and more confused. She started feeling neglected, as Nishant was away for work, and Neelima was at home but busy with her newborn. Once Laika tried to jump on the bed to see what was inside that bundle, but she was scolded badly. From then on Laika became a very quiet and sad dog. She kept lying on the ground all day as if there was no energy left in her.

Laika woke up to a panic one morning. The baby was crying and coughing very badly, and Neelima was panicking. Nishant was not home. Neelima rushed her baby to her pediatrician. He checked the baby up and said – *Nothing to worry, Mrs. Kapoor. She is fine! Take her home.*

But at home, the baby was not fine. She kept crying and coughing, and going red in the face. So, Neelima and Nishant took her to the pediatrician again.

- *Doctor, my baby is not* ***fine****!* – said Nishant. – *At home she cries and coughs, and her face gets red! Although, here she seems fine! Believe me, doc. We are* ***not*** *paranoid.*

Doctor Manish Kumar thought for a while, and asked – *Do you by chance have a cat or dog at home? Any pets?*

Neelima and Nishant looked at each-other.

- *Yes,* – they said together, - *a dog!*

- *Then,* ***there's*** *your problem!* – said the doctor. Seeing confused looks on their faces, the doctor elaborated – *One reason why your baby seems cranky at home, but fine in a hospital might be that she is allergic to dogs or dog hair! Babies have small, not fully-developed lungs, you see.*

- *What should we do then, doc?* – asked Nishant.

- *Get rid of the dog!* – the doctor simply said.

- *But, she is like our daughter,* - said Neelima.

- *It's either the dog or your baby!* – said the doctor heartlessly. He continued – *You see, allergic reactions in babies can be quite severe. If you delay, you might lose....*

- ***No!*** - Neelima cut in – *Don't say such things. The dog goes!*

The very next day transport was arranged and a man was hired to take Laika to Nishant's parents' house in another town, His father was a military man, and so he had many dogs while he was serving in the army, and Nishant practically grew up with them. So, when Nishant and Neelima requested them, they were more than happy to welcome Laika in to their home. There Laika stayed till the last day of her life!

After Laika was sent away, Nishant and Neelima's baby - Mehak, got better. Everyone was glad, well...every *human*, that is. Laika was very sad and kept waiting for her '*mom*' to come soon and pick her up. Laika dreamt of her '*parents*', their house, even their baby, and saw herself playing with them in their house. But, after a few years of waiting, Laika gave up. It is then when she started getting sick.

* * *

It was a chilly November morning. Neelima was tossing and turning in her bed. She was dreaming about Laika after so many years. In her dream she saw Laika roaming around in the house playfully as she used to when she was staying with them. Neelima was sitting on the bed sipping tea. Suddenly, Laika came to her bedside and stood there just looking at her. Neelima put her hand on Laika's head and asked lovingly - *What is it, Laiku?*

Laika didn't respond, just stood there for a while closing her eyes while Neelima stroked her head. She seemed to have been enjoying this affection from her 'mom'. But after sometime Laika suddenly ran out of the room. Neelima kept calling her name - *Laika! Laika! Come back!*

Neelima woke up from her dream breathless. She was sweating and feeling uneasy. She looked at the clock. It was 6 a.m. It was a Sunday. Nishant was still sleeping next to her. Mehak was also sleeping in her crib. Neelima took a sip of water, but the uneasy feeling was not going away. So, she decided to wake Nishant up. She gently patted on his shoulder whispering his name softly - *Nishant! Nishant! Please wake up.*

Nishant looked at her with sleepy eyes and asked - *What is it, Darling? It's a **Sunday**!*

Neelima patted him gently once more - *Nishant! I am not feeling well.*

Nishant sat up on the bed worried – *What happened? You sick?*

Neelima said – *No, no. But, I am feeling uneasy. I dreamt of Laika just now! It felt like she was here, you know. I patted her for some time, but then she just disappeared!*

- *It was just a dream, Baby!* – said Nishant.

- *No, I don't think so. I think something is wrong with Laika! Please call your parents!* – Neelima was sounding worried and anxious.

- *But it's six o'clock in the morning!* – protested Nishant.

- *Your parents get up early! Please, call them and ask!* – Neelima pleaded.

Before Nishant could say anything else, the phone rang! Nishant and Neelima looked at each-other. He picked up the receiver; his father's voice was on the other end.

- *Beta*[27]*, Nishant! There's a bad news for you.*

Nishant's heart started pounding. He swallowed and said – *Ha*[28]*, Papa! What is it?*

- *Laika died today morning at around five-thirty in her sleep.*

Nishant sat dazed in silence! Looking at his face, Neelima got worried – *What happened, Honey?*

- *What time did you say you had the dream about Laika?* – he just uttered in a dazed voice.

- *At around 5.30 in the morning! Why?* – Neelima asked.

- *Laika died today morning at around 5.30; I think she came to say 'good bye' to you!*

27. Beta - son
28. Ha - Yes

STORY NO. 9

Come with Me!

Sandeep doesn't remember any of this, but his mother used to tell this story about him.

- *It's a **true** story,* - she used to insist.

The story went something like this –

When Sandeep was born he was a premature baby. His birth weight was just about two kilos. Doctors gave him a year's time to survive; that's it! But his mother refused to give up. She treated her baby boy like a normal baby, and as most of us will agree, miracles *do* happen, Sandeep not only survived beyond his first year of life, but he entered into his teen years with full force! He was an energetic boy who loved playing cricket. No one was more proud of him than his mother.

Sandeep's family had almost forgotten about his weak, premature birth, when one night Sandeep's parents' worst fear came true!

It was a hot summer night. Sandeep's parents used to sleep on their house's roof as during summers their house used to heat up. But since they were extra protective of Sandeep, they never let him sleep on the rooftop. His mother worried that he might catch a cold; he might accidentally fall from the roof, and so on. This summer night was no different. Sandeep's parents were sleeping on the rooftop; Sandeep was sleeping in his room down below. His mother was an extra cautious woman, so she locked the doors to their house every night without fail, lest someone might enter it with malicious intentions. She was not much worried about her worldly possessions though; it was Sandeep whose safety worried her. So, as usual, the doors to their house were locked and secured.

In his sleep, Sandeep felt something weighing heavily on his chest. He could not breathe. In his dream, he was running very fast and was short of breath, but he was unable to stop! Suddenly with a jerk he opened his eyes, and what he saw made him freeze in silence! He saw that a white transparent apparition of a womanly-figure was sitting on his chest and looking right at his face! Sandeep tried to scream, but the womanly-figure put her transparent finger on his lips and said in a very melodious, mesmerizing voice – *Shhh…….come with me!*

And she floated up from his chest and started to float away from Sandeep towards the main door of the house. Sandeep was hypnotized. He also got up and started following her as if in his sleep. As they approached the main door of the house, the woman apparition looked back at Sandeep and made a gesture with her right hand's index figure to follow her through the gate. Then she turned towards the gate and floated right through it! Sandeep in a hypnotic state tried to do the same, but his head hit hard on the door which was locked by his mother, and he came out of his stupor. He fell down on the floor and was unconscious!

* * *

- *Sandeep! Sandeep!* – someone was shouting and splattering water on his face. - *Sandeep, wake up!*

Sandeep opened his eyes to see that he was lying on his mother's lap and a small crowd had gathered around them. He looked at a few of them turn-by-turn, and then suddenly got up from his mother's lap. He was still on the ground near the main door where he had fainted last night!

- *Maa!* – he said in a surprised voice, - *what happened?*

- *You tell me,* ***what*** *happened?* – Sandeep's mother asked him in a worried voice.

Sandeep closed his eyes for a while as if to recollect what happened the night before. Then he opened his eyes and got up. Dusting off his clothes, he went inside his room and shut the door. His mother followed him to his room and banged on the door shouting his name –

- *Sandeep! Sandeep! Open the door!*

Go away! – came his voice from inside, - *I want to sleep! I am tired.*

Hearing this, his mother left him alone to sleep and told the others who had gathered at her house hearing her screams to go home. The crowd scattered, but Sandeep's mother kept sitting outside his room's door so that when he opens it, he finds her there.

The door opened at around noon. Sandeep came out of his room with sleepy eyes, and saw his mother dozing in front of his door. He sat down and put his head on his mother's lap. His mother woke up with a jerk calling his name – *Sandeep!*

- *Yes, maa. I am right here!*

- *What happened last night, Bachhey*[29]*?* – asked his mother.

Sandeep hesitated, and then said – *You wouldn't believe me if I told you.*

- *Try me. I am your mother. I will never disbelieve you!* – said his mother.

Sandeep kept quiet for some time, and then narrated the entire incident of last night to his mother. The mother got really worried and scared, as any loving mother would. She in turn narrated the story to her husband. Both of them agreed that this incident cannot be ignored.

Next day Sandeep was taken to a hypnotherapist. Sandeep was unwilling, but when his parents promised that they will be

---

29. Bachhey – a form of the word kid, like kiddo.

by his side the entire time, and the hypnotherapist also permitted it, he agreed. The hypnotherapist made Sandeep lie down on a sofa. She dimmed the lights of the room. Sandeep's mother held his hands, while his father stood in a corner of the room in the dark. The hypnotherapist sat on a chair beside Sandeep. She had a shiny pendant with a chain in her hand. She started swaying it in front of Sandeep and started saying in a calm and soothing voice:

- *Sandeep, look at the pendant. Feel the rhythm. Try to relax.*

Sandeep kept looking at the swaying pendant, and the more he looked at it, the heavier his eyelids became. He started drifting; he could still hear the faint voice of the hypnotherapist:

- *Sandeep, are you asleep?*

- *Hmm...*, Sandeep moaned.

- *Tell me, Sandeep, where are you now?*

- *Jodhpur*, - came the reply.

Sandeep's mother looked at the hypnotherapist with a worried look on her face and opened her mouth to say something, but the hypnotherapist put her index finger to her mouth to gesture her to keep quiet. Sandeep's father came near her slowly trying not to make much sound, and calmly kept his hand on her shoulder. This calmed her down.

The hypnotherapist continued – *Sandeep, what year is it?*

There was a silent moment, then Sandeep said in a different, deeper voice than his – *I am **not** Sandeep. I am Raghu, and this is 1957.*

Sandeep's parents exchanged a look with each-other, and then they both looked at the therapist. She raised her hand in the air as if to tell them that – *it's ok.* She then looked back at Sandeep and said – *What are you doing now, **Raghu**?*

The questioning angered Sandeep, and he shouted at the therapist:

- *Keep quiet, woman! Don't disturb me! I have to teach my wife a lesson!*

And Sandeep started making gestures with his hands as if he is beating and thrashing someone! Sandeep's parents were horrified seeing their meek and shy son in such an aggressive mood. There was a crooked smile on Sandeep's face. He looked extremely satisfied. He blurted out:

- ***There!*** *That'll teach you a lesson never to disobey me!* – then after a few seconds he spoke again, this time taking someone's name: - *Meena,* ***Meena****! Wake up! Meena!*

The expression on Sandeep's face suddenly changed from that of satisfaction to confusion to being horrified. He exclaimed – *Oh, no! I* ***killed*** *her!* He gasped for air – *What should I do now? Oh, God! Oh, God!* Sandeep started panting and squirming in his sleep. Sandeep's mother wanted to soothe him, but the therapist stopped her and signaled to – *wait*!

Sandeep kept blabbering – *Where to hide her body? Where? Where?*

Then suddenly he started digging. He dug for a while and then suddenly stopped. He was panting and was sweaty from the hard work. He wiped his sweat from his forehead and said in a strangely relieved voice – *I think this pit is good enough! She is a small woman, she will fit in it! No one will ever find out that I buried her right in the middle of our* ***house****!* And Sandeep started laughing a devilish laugh.

The hypnotherapist snapped her fingers in front of Sandeep's ears, and Sandeep suddenly woke up as if from a trance. He looked at the horrified faces of the three people in the room. He turned towards his mother – *Maa, what happened? Why are you all looking at me like* ***that****?*

- *Nothing, beta. It's ok. Just relax!* – His mother replied. Then she looked at the hypnotherapist. She nodded her head.

- *Sandeep,* - asked the hypnotherapist – *how are you feeling?*

- *I am perfectly fine,* - replied Sandeep a bit surprised.

- *Then you may get up from the sofa, and relax!* – said the hypnotherapist. – *Just sit here for some time.* Then she looked at the parents and gestured them to go out of the room with her eyes. The parents silently left the room. The hypnotherapist said to Sandeep – *You were in a deep slumber, so just sit for a while. Don't get up suddenly. I will just come back in a moment. She came outside the room where his parents were waiting impatiently.* The moment they saw her they exclaimed – *What does this* ***mean****, doctor?*

- Sandeep went into his past life, as it seems...he was a different person and it was a different time! It's more than 50 years now! So, don't worry about it too much. As a therapist what I can say is that the apparition that he saw might be his dead wife Meena. I suggest you bring him to me for more sessions; maybe I can get rid of his past life's guilt. His subconscious still remembers what happened.

The parents looked confused, so the hypnotherapist added – *Look, the human mind is very complex and it works on so many different levels....these type of things are hard to explain, and even harder to digest...but I have seen in my profession stranger things. Don't worry, with therapy he will be alright.*

- But, why is this dead wife coming back now??? What does she want? Does she want to punish him? Revenge, perhaps. Is my son safe? – Sandeep's mother had so many questions.

- Look, don't worry too much about it. Maybe she is coming back now because this was his age in his previous life when he...you know, killed her...there can be lot more reasons. Just let me get to know Sandeep a bit better.

In the next couple of sessions the hypnotherapist found out that this Meena had come back to haunt him with the purpose of taking his life the same way he had taken hers in the previous life. Meena had died at the same age at which Sandeep was now. She swore that she would ***not*** rest in peace till she killed him and took him away with her!

This greatly frightened the parents. They decided to take Sandeep to a *tantric*[30]. The *tantric* suggested a way to get rid of the curse that had fallen upon Sandeep. They have to find out the house of this Raghu and dig its courtyard and remove Meena's

30. Tantric – one who uses tantra-mantra (meditation, rituals) etc. to heal people. Though these days they are judged harshly.

corpse and give it a proper Hindu death ritual by burning her body on a funeral pyre. Then only her spirit would leave this world peacefully.

The very next day Sandeep's parents booked train tickets for Jodhpur and started looking for Raghu and Meena's house. They eventually tracked down a small village around Jodhpur where lived an old man who claimed to be a hundred years old! He heard the name *Raghu* and *Meena,* and almost jumped out of his chair. He said that after Meena's disappearance, Raghu was heart-broken and he died a very sad man. This old man even managed to point out Raghu's house to Sandeep's parents, and also warned them that it is haunted. It was a dilapidated, abandoned house that lay in shambles.

That night Sandeep's parents took lanterns and spades to this old house and started digging. To their utter surprise they found a petite woman's remains in the middle of the house's courtyard. It was a dark night and a creepy feeling came over Sandeep's parents as if someone's watching them. They wrapped the body in a sack and took it to the cremation grounds nearby. There was no one there that night. So, Sandeep's parents built a funeral pyre with wood from the mango trees which were growing around the cremation ground, and Sandeep's father performed her last rites and burnt her remains praying for her soul to rest in peace.

Miraculously, after that night Sandeep never saw that apparition again in his life!

STORY NO. 10

Hauntings of the Previous Life

Sumeet was an introvert since childhood. He was a brilliant boy, but was shy and liked to keep his thoughts to himself. His elder sister Ramona was an extrovert. She was bold, and she loved talking to people. Sumeet adored her sister but he never looked at her straight; he always looked at her feet while talking to her.

Since Sumeet was scared of dark, he and his sister shared a room. Their mother made them sleep on the same bed even though Ramona wanted a room of her own telling her that she is his elder sister and she needs to take care of her weak younger brother.

Many a nights Sumeet used to wake up screaming in the middle of the night. Mother used to come running to their room.

- *What happened, Su?* – She used to take him in her arms and calm him.

- *Mom, his screaming disturbs my sleep!* – Ramona used to complain.

- *Ramona, you have to take care of him! He is your baby brother.* – Mother used to scold her.

- *Maa, ...*- Sumeet used to say softly in a scared voice, - *Maa, somebody was pulling my blanket!*

- *What!* – Ramona used to get irritated, - *Mom, I am sleeping in the **same** blanket, no one pulled mine! See, **this** is why I need a separate room!*

- *Ramona, keep quiet! Not everything is about **you**!* – Mother used to shut her up.

Ramona used to hold her brother's hands and take him to school every day. Most days Sumeet would be too scared to go to school. Some days he vomited while going to school, and Ramona had to bring him back home. As a result either she missed school or was late for school.

One day Ramona came back from school and she felt an eerie silence upon entering her house. She looked around and called out for her mother – "*Maa...*"

Her mother came out of Ramona's room looking gloomy with tears in her eyes. Ramona got worried – *What happened, Maa?*

Mother replied in short – *Your brother is not well.*

Ramona rushed inside her room and saw her brother lying helplessly on the bed on his back and staring at the ceiling. She waited for him to blink, but he didn't! He kept staring at the ceiling. Ramona came to his bedside and touched his forehead; it was burning up! She rushed out and said to mother – *Maa, he **needs** to be taken to a hospital! Did you call Paa??*

Her mother shook her head negatively. Ramona picked up the phone and dialed her father's office number. After a full set of ringing the phone just stopped. No one had picked up the phone from the other end. This irritated Ramona. Why only during emergencies *this* happens!

Mother said calmly, in a sad voice – *We just have to wait for your father to come home in the evening.*

Ramona was not happy. But she had no choice. She had a test tomorrow and she has to study for it. But her brother was in their room and not well. So, she took her schoolbag to the rooftop and decided to study there.

Father came home around six in the evening. Ramona heard his car. She rushed down and shouted at her father – *We were trying to reach you at the office, but no one picked up our call! Where were you, Paa?*

- *What's the emergency, Ramona?* – he said dryly.

- *It was an emergency! Sumeet was burning up with fever!* – Ramona almost screamed.

Father went inside the room and checked Sumeet's forehead. – *The fever seems to have subsided. He is just sleeping now. Let him* ***be!***

Ramona threw up her arms in the air and went back to her studies.

It was quite late when she came down for dinner. She didn't particularly feel like eating dinner with her 'dysfunctional' family that evening. She heated up her food and ate quietly alone. Her parents had gone to sleep. After dinner she went to her room thinking where to sleep tonight? When she entered the room it was dark. She could not see a thing for a while. When her eyes eventually adjusted to the darkness, she realized that Sumeet was not on the bed. She checked the bathroom. He wasn't there as well.

- *Where could he* ***be*** *at this hour?* – Ramona thought.

Suddenly she felt a cold breeze in the room and then she noticed that the back door to their room was a bit ajar! Ramona was alarmed. She hesitatingly opened the door and peeked out. What she saw gave her the chills! Her sick brother was lying in the middle of an empty plot on the ground on his back and was continuously staring at the sky. Ramona started shouting for her parents – ***Maa…Papa!*** *Come quick!*

She waited for her parents to come. Her parents who were not very fast asleep because of Sumeet not being well heard their daughter calling for them and came running to her room. They saw Ramona standing at the back door.

- *Ramona, what is it?* – Her mother asked and came running towards her. Father also followed. Ramona pointed out towards the empty plot. As they looked on they saw their son lying there on the ground.

- ***Su***! – Mother ran towards him, father also ran with mother. They reached where he was lying motionless with his eyes open. Mother lifted his head and kept it on her lap crying. Father also sat beside mother. Sumeet suddenly came alive and pointing towards the sky started repeating – *They came to get me! They came to get me!*

- **Who?** – asked mother with tears in her eyes.

- *Who came to take you?* – asked father firmly.

But Sumeet was not listening to them He was in a stupor. He continued – T*hey called my name….I followed them….but, they…. they didn't wait for me! They floated up to the sky….I ran as fast as I could….but couldn't float up!* And Sumeet started sobbing. Mother and father exchanged a glance and then called his name, but Sumeet did not respond. Ramona was still standing at the back door horrified.

Father called his name again, this time more intensely, and then he slapped Sumeet to bring him out of his stupor. Mother made a painful sound, but kept holding Sumeet. After the slap Sumeet looked at his father and then mother and started crying.

This incident scared every member of the family. Mother never left Sumeet alone; Ramona wasn't allowed to go to school for a few days so that when mother went to the bathroom or kitchen she could be at her brother's bedside.

After a few days father came home from office and said to mother – *Listen, I have found out about one hypnotherapist through a colleague of mine in office. Apparently, he is a very efficient man. We need to take Sumeet there. His…uh…behavior is not normal. We don't understand what he keeps mumbling about!*

- *What…who is a 'hypnotherapist'?* – mother asked doubtfully.

- *Someone who will make sense out of all of this and will be able to explain our son's situation* – father replied curtly. He continued – *Tomorrow, I will take an appointment and we will go to him as soon as possible.*

The whole family ate dinner quietly and went to bed.

The day after father took an appointment and the whole

family went to meet this hypnotherapist. Ramona was curious. She never heard about a hypnotherapist before. Mother was not very comfortable, and Sumeet was scared as always! As they sat in the reception, they looked around. The office was tastefully decorated, and there was no one else other than them. A woman came to inform them that the '*doctor*' is ready for them. Hearing the word '*doctor*' put mother at ease. – *Oh, so he is a doctor!* – she thought with relief.

As they all entered the room, they saw that it was a dimly-lit room. Curtains were drawn over the windows and a figure was sitting at the far end of the room behind a desk. There were a few chairs in the room and a couch in the middle of the room. As they tried to figure out the '*doctor's*' face, they heard a deep voice, - Please come, sit.

They all sat down facing the hypnotherapist quietly and stared at him doubtfully. Sumeet was as usual looking down. The deep voice came again – *So…over the phone I spoke with you, Mr. Gupta?*

- *That's me,* - father lifted one arm like students do at school in front of the teacher.

- *You can keep your hands down* – the hypnotherapist smiled. – *This must be Sumeet, then.* He said looking at him. Sumeet did not lift his eyes. – *It's ok, Sumeet. You can look at me.* His voice was so deep and soothing that Sumeet looked up at him. – *Don't be scared, my child. Nothing here is going to cause you pain. I am not that kind of a 'doctor'.*

- *What will you do to me?* – Sumeet asked fearfully.

- *Nothing, just talk! I promise.* – The hypnotherapist replied. – *Now, Sumeet, if you don't mind, would you lie down on that couch?* – The hypnotherapist requested. Sumeet quietly got up from his chair and lay down on the couch. Mother looked worried, but before she could ask anything, the '*doctor*' calmed her down – *Mrs. Gupta, please don't worry. I am just going to make him sleep and then in his sleep he will tell me what's bothering him! You see, sometimes a person doesn't open up when he is awake!*

- *He is going to talk in his sleep?* – the mother was confused.

- *Don't worry, Mrs. Gupta. You can all be present here. But, make sure* ***not*** *to interrupt before the session is over.* - Hypnotherapist warned.

They all nodded, and took chairs at the far corner of the room and sat in the dark. Sumeet was restless, so the *'doctor'* said - *'Sumeet, it's ok. They all are here.* ***See!*** Sumeet saw the faint figures of his family members in the dark, and that calmed him down a bit.

- *Sumeet, now look at me and then close your eyes and listen to* ***only*** *my voice.* - said the hypnotherapist. Sumeet nodded and closed his eyes. It seemed that he fell asleep in no time and the hypnotherapist was saying something that sounded like he was chanting or humming. Then suddenly there was silence! Ramona wanted to swallow, but was too scared to, lest the sound of her swallowing disturbs the session!

- *Sumeet* - the hypnotherapist called his name. After about ten seconds he called his name again, gently – ***Sumeet!***

A strange unknown voice of a grown man entered everyone's ears in that room – *There is* **NO** *Sumeet here!*

Everyone but the hypnotherapist gasped. Hypnotherapist just lifted his left arm so that the family members remain quiet. He asked lovingly – *Then* **Who** *are you?*

After about ten seconds the deep male voice replied – *I am Raja.*

- *Where do you live, Raja?* – the hypnotherapist asked politely.

There was silence. Then came the sound of deep breathing, followed by sobbing. Next what the family heard scared them for life! The deep sad male voice replied – *I am* **not** *alive anymore. My wife – Roopa and her lover murdered me in my sleep! I was sitting in Heaven for a long time NOT wanting to come back to Earth, but…but God has decided to send me back to earth! I am too scared to live among people, and especially, I DON'T trust women!*

The male voice started sobbing. The hypnotherapist said very soothingly – *It's ok, Raja. You can go back to sleep now. When you wake up, the world would be a better place.*

Everyone was just sitting stunned for a few minutes. Then the hypnotherapist got up from his chair, switched-on the lights and went back and sat at his table as before when the family had entered the room. He looked at the scared faces of the family and called them to approach him by gesturing with his fingers. Mother stopped Ramona from coming. The parents approached the hypnotherapist.

- *Ask your daughter to take her brother outside this room when he wakes up.*

Ramona heard that and nodded. As she approached her brother, she noticed that he is awake. In a feeble voice Sumeet asked – *What happened, Di? Where's mom?*

- *Everybody is here. Your treatment is done. The doctor is prescribing medicines for you. Mom and dad are there, see. Now, let's get up. We will sit outside for a while.*

When the brother and sister left the room, the hypnotherapist said to the parents – *I know, it's hard to believe such stuff....but this is a case of* ***rebirth****! Your son's soul is a scared, dissatisfied soul that has trust issues especially with women. He vividly remembers his last day... he remembers being* ***murdered****!*

STORY NO. 11

The Dying Wish

A great visionary had once said that - ***dreams are not what you see after you fall asleep; dreams are what do NOT let you sleep at night.*** So True!

Meenu's father was a great writer. But his field of interest was Chess. Though he published a couple of books on Chess in his lifetime, Meenu was not aware of these. Actually, other than the father no one in that family liked or understood Chess.

One day when Meenu came back from college, her father called her - *Meenu*!

It was strange because her father never interacted much with the family. After retirement he just kept to himself and kept himself occupied with Chess. She had just climbed up the first step of the staircase when she heard her father call her name. She started walking towards her father's room. On the way she saw her mom glancing from the kitchen. Meenu asked her by hand gesture as to why father is calling her? Her mom just gave a shrug, and got busy in the kitchen. Meenu's heart started thumping harder as she approached her father's room.

She peeked in and said - *Yes, papa*?

Her father gestured with his hand - *Come, sit with me.*

Meenu was now even more worried - *Is something the matter, papa?*

He looked up from his books and said in a serious manner - *You have to take me to a good hospital tomorrow.*

Meenu's heart skipped a beat - *What happened to you?*

Father replied calmly - *It's alright. Are you free tomorrow?*

Meenu said - *I have one class, but this is more important. I can skip it.*

There was an awkward silence for some time. Meenu just kept standing there. Father looked up from his study table and asked - *Anything else?*

- *You tell me that! You can't just say something like this and not give an explanation!* - Meenu blurted out. - *What happened to you?*

Father calmly took a big X-ray film and showed it to Meenu. Meenu glanced at it and asked - *What is it?*

- *Our family doctor took these a couple of days ago. Today I went back to see him, and he advised that I should visit a good pulmonologist.*

- *Pulm...what?* - Meenu couldn't even pronounce it.

- *It's my lungs, Dear. There's something not right with them. Our family doctor asked me to get a second opinion. That's all.* - Meenu's father replied, and went back to studying.

Meenu dashed to the kitchen where her mother was making tea. She blurted out - *Mom, what's this about? Papa never liked going to the hospital....and now he is insisting!*

Mom replied - *When has your father* ***ever*** *explained something? Honey, just google a good doctor and take him there.*

Mom saw Meenu lost in thoughts, so said calmly - *Sweetie, when has your father* ***ever*** *asked for your help? Just do it.*

Meenu went up to her bedroom and found a good hospital with a reputed pulmonologist and booked the appointment, but the worry never let her sleep that night. She kept tossing and turning in her bed. In the morning after breakfast they set out for that hospital. It was not very far from their house. Both kept silent during the travel.

- *Mr. Kishor Yadav*! – Meenu heard her father's name being called. She jumped up and said – *Yes! That's us.*

Doctor was a sympathetic-looking middle-aged man. He listened to Meenu's father attentively and looked at the X-ray. Although Meenu was present in the room, she constantly kept looking out the window.

She heard the doctor say – *Mr. Yadav. We are going to admit you for a day or two to run some more tests.* This got Meenu's attention. She looked at the doctor – *Is everything ok?*

- *We'll see.* – The doctor replied. Then he called out some name. A male nurse entered. Doctor said to Meenu – *He will take care of all the formalities. Come back after a few days. And, don't worry, your father is in good hands!*

* * *

- *Your father has fourth stage lung cancer* – Meenu could not believe her ears! The doctor continued – *There's nothing much we can do. He is too old for chemo. We can try radiation therapy. Ms. Meenu....are you* ***listening****?*

Meenu got up and ran out of the room. She went to the bathroom and started crying. Her father was a heavy smoker. She kind of suspected that this would eventually happen! But, now that it's happening, it's too much to cope with. She splashed some water on to her face, calmed herself down, and entered the doctor's room – *I'm so sorry!*

- *Don't worry. I understand.* The doctor replied.

- *How long does he have*? – Meenu asked the 'difficult' question bluntly.

- *Maybe a few months.* After a pause he added – *You can keep him comfortable at home. I don't think radiation is going to help that much. I will prepare the discharge slip. You can go get your father ready.*

Meenu got up in a hurry, thanked the doctor and went straight to her father's hospital room. He was awake. She managed a smile, and said – *Papa, let's take you home!*

* * *

The atmosphere at home was gloomy. Mom was crying in her room, trying to be as silent as possible. Meenu called her younger brother who lived in South Africa. He promised to book a ticket as soon as possible. Father was very quiet amidst this commotion. He quietly got up from sofa and went to his room, and closed the door. Everyone got worried. Meenu and her mom kept knocking on the door, begging for him to open it. After some time, father opened the door. He was carrying a thick folder in his hands.

- *Meenu beta,* - he called out to her.

Meenu went to him and sat down beside him. After a few silent minutes, her father said to her with tears in his eyes. - *I know. I am very ill. I insisted, and the doctor told me. Don't pain yourself over this. I had a good life, good house, good job, great life partner and children. You all kept telling me to quit smoking, I didn't listen…and now this! I brought it upon myself. I have made my peace with it.*

He paused to take a breath. Meenu noticed he was struggling for it. She held his hand and began crying. – *Don't cry, baby. All my wishes have come true. I am a happy man. Just…..,* and he paused again.

Meenu looked at him – *Yes, papa? Just…what?*

He took out the folder from under his arm and handed it over to Meenu. He said – *I know, you people think that I love Chess more than all of you….and maybe you are right. I am sorry for neglecting you all….,* and he shut his eyes tight. Meenu saw a tear roll down his eyes. Meenu never saw her father cry! He opened his eyes and handed Meenu his folder saying – *This is my life's work. I am gifting it to you. You have to promise me that you will fulfill my last wish…. my dying wish!*

* * *

Meenu's father passed away a few months later. The household went into a depressive silence after that. No one was really the same….it happens when you lose a loved one, and that too the head of the family. Meenu was clueless and lost for a while. She was so heart-broken that she had forgotten all about her father's dying wish and his manuscript.

Soon after her father's passing Meenu started having the same dream over-and-over again. Her father would appear in her dream looking sad and gloomy, and would just sit beside her in her bed and stare at her with a question in his eyes! Meenu tried to open her mouth and speak to her father, but no words would come out of her mouth. In panic, she would wake up! This went on for a year!

Meenu had no idea why she was having these dreams? Is it that she has not been able to let go of her father? With each passing day she got more and more convinced about it. She confided in a friend at work. The friend suggested her to visit a therapist, one that is an expert in dream interpretations. This made sense to Meenu, and she did.

During her first session with the therapist she narrated her recurring dream. Therapist calmed her down and asked her to relax.

- *There must be a reason that your father is appearing in your dreams....*- the therapist said. After a pause he continued – *Tell me, Meenu, how does your father look in your dreams? I mean, does he look happy, or sad...or...*

Before the therapist could finish his query, Meenu blurted out – *he looks really sad....and as if he has a question for me...*

- *Hmm...*brooded the therapist. Then after a pause he said – *I think, he has some unfinished business....that which is related to you...*

- *unfinished business...related to me...*Meenu repeated the phrase.

- *Yes, like a wish that is still unfulfilled....*the moment the therapist uttered these words, Meenu jumped up from her chair and said excitedly – *Oh My God! How could I forget....his dying wish....he wanted me to publish his manuscript...his last finished manuscript!*

Meenu left the therapists office a happy woman. She thanked him with her whole heart, and went straight to work to fulfill her father's last wish. She found a Chess Publisher online. She contacted them; to her surprise they knew her father and his work! They were sad to hear of his demise, and readily agreed to publish his last manuscript along with an obituary page as a tribute to her father.

Finally, after about a year, her father's last Chess book was published. That night she slept like a baby with a smile on her face. Her father never came to her dreams again looking sad.

STORY NO. 12

The Call from Beyond

They say that there is nothing after death, that death is the final destination! I used to believe the same!

Mr. Dey was an atheist. Well, not exactly. He was a good man, earning a good living, and he used to say that – *I don't deny that there is God, but I don't **need** him!* He used to say that people do not worship God because of their love and devotion for Him; people worship God because they *need* something from Him! His family always found this attitude of his strange and unacceptable.

Mr. Dey supported his family well, financially and otherwise and retired from a good post. The entire family was celebrating his retirement thinking that now he would be able to devote more time to his family. Everything went well for a while.

Then one fine day as Mr. Dey was returning from the market, he felt a strange pain rising in his chest, and he collapsed on the pavement, not very far from his house. A neighbor spotted him. An ambulance was called and he was immediately taken to a hospital. Doctors told his family that he had had a mild heart attack.

After a few days stay in the hospital Mr. Dey came home. His family took great care of him as they all loved him. Mr. Dey was enjoying the attention. His wife gave him his favorite food; his teenage children – one son and one daughter were always by his side. Mr. Dey didn't want anything else.

One day he called his entire family and requested – *I know it's hard for you to give up your cell phones, but I just need a couple of hours from you....your undivided attention. You can suggest the time and day for that. Make all your calls and stuff....then switch off your mobiles just for a couple of hours.*

His family was worried and curious at the same time. Hence they set a date and time, and on that date and time they switched off their cell phones and sat with Mr. Dey in his room. The look on their worried faces made Mr. Dey chuckle. – *Why are all of you so morose? I am not gone, yet!*

Mrs. Dey said in a concerned voice – *Please, don't say such a thing! What is it that you wanted to tell us?*

Mr. Dey took a deep breath and began –

*My life wasn't always this good...**you** know Meera,* he said to his wife, - *but my children don't. Today I want to narrate my whole life to them. They should know about their father's life, his struggles.....* Saying this Mr. Dey closed his eyes as if to recollect his entire life in his mind. The children were looking at him, and waiting in silence for him to start his story.

Slowly Mr. Dey opened his eyes and started – *I wasn't always Mr. Dey, you know...I had a pet name – Nitai. My mother used to call me that....I lost my mother pretty early!* Mr. Dey sighed, and then continued – *Soon after my father left us....it was just my younger brother and I...we were just seven and nine...*

Mr. Dey's children knew about their *kaku*[31]. He had died a couple of years back, but till the time he was alive he was devoted to Mr. Dey! He followed every word of his elder brother, and loved him immensely, since Mr. Dey had supported them both right from their childhood. He worked at a matchbox factory during the day and studied under a street light by the night.

31. Kaku – Father's younger brother in Bangla

His younger brother followed in his footsteps. They both turned out to be exceptional students, and after finishing school went to good colleges with scholarships. Both of them bagged good government jobs.

Both were lucky to have good families, and were happy. But suddenly one day a few years before his retirement *kaku* fell violently ill, and after a few days suffering, he passed away! This had given quite a shock to Mr. Dey, as he kept mumbling now and then after that - *I should have gone first....I was the eldest!*

He never really recovered from the shock of losing his baby brother. And then he retired. And this thought of his brother dying before him kept haunting him since now he had plenty of free time. And after Mr. Dey fell ill, he kept thinking about his brother and their difficult childhood. That was the story he wanted to tell his children.

After his story was over, the children kept sitting in silence for a moment with tears in their eyes. The stupor was broken by their mother – *It's ok, kids. Come let's have tea together as a family, and celebrate this time we have together.*

That night Mr. Dey felt uneasy. He kept falling in and out of sleep. He was staring at the dark lying on his bed when suddenly he saw a movement. As he strained his eyes to see in the darkness he heard a familiar voice - *Nitai Da*[32]*!*

Mr. Dey's eyes widened with shock as he saw his younger brother...his *dead* younger brother standing at the doorway to his bedroom! Mr. Dey shouted out his name - *Nirmal! Bhai!*[33] *Don't go...don't leave me again!*

The shouting woke his wife and children up. - *What happened? You must have seen a bad dream!* – his wife said.

- *It wasn't a dream*! - Mr. Dey shouted, his arm still outstretched for his brother. - *Nirmal had come! He called out to me! He is here! He is here to take me with him!*

32. Da – Short form for elder brother in Bangla
33. Bhai – younger brother

Everyone in his family got scared. The family doctor was called in an emergency. Mr. Dey was burning with fever; he was falling in and out of consciousness. He seemed delirious. Mrs. Dey was in tears, his children were in shock.

Two days Mr. Dey slept like a baby. It was dusk when he woke up from his sleep. Mrs. Dey gave him some hot tea to sip. He was sitting on the sofa in the drawing room with his children. He finished his tea, kept it on the table, and then to everyone's shock said - *Nirmal is here too...Meera, give him some tea, please.* And he pointed to an empty sofa. - *Can't you see...he is sitting right there! He was waiting for me to finish my tea....he knows how much I love sipping hot tea!*

Everyone stared at the empty sofa. Mr. Dey said - *Let's go, brother. Everything is fine here. My family is taken care of.*

Before anyone could react to that, Mr. Dey stretched out his arms towards the empty sofa, and in a flash his Soul left his body, as his lifeless body fell back to the sofa! The last sentence he uttered was - *Oh, God!*

STORY NO. 13

The Voice

Did anyone of you ever experience such an acoustic phenomenon where you *think* you have heard a voice which in fact wasn't audible to anyone else? Well, my mother did, and she still tells this miraculous story to everyone.

It happened a long time back, when I was still in college. My mother had this habit...well, more like her forgetfulness...she would keep something to cook on gas, and then forget about it until a burning smell reached our noses.

It was neither afternoon nor evening. None of us were home, other than my mother who is a housewife. My father was in his office, at his workplace; my brothers were at school; I was at my University, had classes till five in the evening.

That day my mother had a cold. Since she was not feeling like eating normal food alone, she decided to make *kheer*[34] for all of us. She kept a litre of milk on the gas for boiling, which is usually the first step of preparing this rice dish. Suddenly the phone in her bedroom rang...and *yes,* those days there were no cellphones. It

34. Kheer – sweet dish made of milk, rice and sugar

was my mother's childhood friend, Renu. She was calling from Kolkata. She was calling after a long time, and my mother got so engrossed in this telephonic conversation that she forgot all about the milk! It was a litre of milk, kept on slow flame, so it took quite some time to boil over. But, eventually, it did.

There was no burning smell as the milk did not burn, it spilt over and extinguished the flame. The kitchen was at the other end of the house, so the smell of LPG[35] didn't reach my mother's nose, so to speak. To add to this, my mother had a blocked nose that day, a sign of an oncoming cold.

My mother finished her conversation with her childhood friend, and kept the receiver down. She was in a good mood and was humming the tune of her favorite song. She was happy because her childhood friend just invited all of us to her son's wedding. She couldn't wait to give us the news. She proceeded towards the kitchen. She was about to switch on the light of the kitchen when she heard my voice screaming - *Mom, DON'T....*

She was stupefied! She called out my name - *Mona, is that you? Are you back from your classes?* Saying this she entered my bedroom. To her surprise, it was empty! Then she peeked inside the washroom to check whether I am there. I was not!

She searched for me in the entire house, and in the garden that was surrounding our house. She couldn't find me anywhere! Surprised, she went back inside the house. Suddenly she remembered that she is forgetting something. - *What is it that I am forgetting?* - she kept mumbling.

Meanwhile, I reached home and immediately smelt the strong stench of the LPG that was leaking from the gas cylinder which was still in '**on**' position. The flames were extinguished by the spilt milk, but the gas stove knob was still on! I rushed to the kitchen and switched the gas knob off.

My mother saw me and was relieved - *Oh, there you are! I had just heard you a few minutes ago. You were trying to stop me from*

35. LPG – Liquified Petroleum Gas used for cooking in households

switching on the kitchen light! I have been looking for you everywhere! Where were you?

- *What are you saying, Mom! I just reached home from college! The gas stove was on, and the milk was spilt over! It was reeking of LPG! Where were you? What were you doing!* – I almost shouted at her.

She suddenly remembered what she was forgetting - *Oh, Lord! I had kept milk for boiling on the gas stove, and then your Renu*[36] *mashi called, and I forgot all about it!*

Then after a brief pause she exclaimed - *Oh, God! I was about to switch on the light to the kitchen, when I heard you shouting at me – no, mom! You saved a big mishap from happening....I could have blown up the entire house...I could have died today! The switching on of the light could have ignited a spark and that could have blown up the leaking LPG cylinder!* The realization of a big tragedy averted had suddenly dawned upon my mother! Had she not heard my '*voice*' that day, she could have died!

Since that day my mother had a new found respect for me... an awe of me...she still says that I am psychic, that I have special powers. But beliefs apart, we all have such incidences happening in and around us. We just have to look for them, sense them. The '*miracle*' that we wait for in our lives, might just have passed us by unnoticed!

I once heard somewhere that every man that dies has a story that dies with him....explore that story before it's too late!

---

36. Mashi – maternal aunt in Bangla